MW00448441

Essential Question
How can learning about nature be useful?

BY DIANA NOONAN
ILLUSTRATED BY CHERYL COOK

CHAPTER 1
BEYOND THE CAVE

"Do you have your life jackets on, everyone?" asked Mr. Prentice.

Elle checked the zipper on her life jacket for the third time. It was not that she was apprehensive about being in the wilderness—she was just worried about how useful this camping trip was going to be for their drama studies.

Mr. Prentice had arrived at school at the start of the month. Although Elle's class had been looking forward to having a new drama teacher, Mr. Prentice had not been quite what they'd imagined. He was kind and understanding, and funny too, but he did not exactly do a lot of drama. In two more weeks, the class would have to perform a play they had written

themselves. So far, though, Mr. Prentice had not even organized a brainstorming session—and now here they were on a canoe trip!

"C'mon, Elle," called Hoover, passing her a paddle. "Let's get moving."

"Look, kids," called Mr. Prentice when they reached the riverbank. "See the turtle hiding in the mud?"

Elle frowned. Ever since they had arrived, Mr. Prentice had been pointing out all the wildlife. She wished he were as interested in drama.

"Okay," said Mr. Prentice. "Take a seat in the canoe, and leave one at the rear for me." When they were all seated, he asked, "Do you all remember the paddling routine? Vanessa, please demonstrate."

"Sure!" replied Vanessa, gesturing energetically. "You make fists like a boxer around the handle of the paddle and then pull back like this."

"Great performance, Vanessa!" said Elle. "Maybe we could feature a canoe in our play." She looked hopefully at Mr. Prentice, but he did not respond. Instead he remarked, "The water here is calm, but it won't be like this the whole way."

"It won't?" squeaked Marta.

"This *is* white-water territory," Hoover chimed in. "We need a challenge!"

"Yes," agreed Mr. Prentice, "but not *too* much, which is why you need to listen carefully. Just beyond the first bend are some rapids, and you'll immediately see a fork in the river. It's very important that we don't take the left-hand fork. That's where we might encounter some problems."

Just then, everyone's attention turned to the water. A large log floated past with a heron perched on it.

"What a magnificent sight!" exclaimed Mr. Prentice. "Aren't we fortunate to be out in nature?"

The group headed downstream in the canoe, but a mere ten minutes later, Mr. Prentice's words echoed in Elle's mind as they again spied that same log. The heron was now standing on a nearby rock, and the log it had been riding was jammed across the main branch of the river!

"What do we do now?" asked Hoover.

"If we steer clear of the log, we'll be pushed down the wrong fork of the river!" cried Marta.

"We have no choice," answered their teacher. "We can't hit the log, and we can't let the current push us up against the cliff. Paddle!"

Elle felt as if she were in a movie being played on fast-forward. One minute they were paddling, the next minute the canoe had overturned.

"Help!" she called, bobbing downstream like a cork.

"Try and stay together!" shouted Mr. Prentice.

Before Elle could do anything, she and Vanessa were dragged into a narrow crevice in the cliff. It was pitch black, and she shut her eyes as the water swirled her around and around.

"This is the end!" thought Elle, but just at that moment, daylight returned, and a strong arm reached out and hauled her toward the shore.

"Got you!" said Mr. Prentice. "Elle, Vanessa, Marta? Are you all okay? Hoover?"

"I'm here," Hoover reassured him. "We're all here."

But as they looked around them at the steep-sided, mist-enshrouded valley, no one could be quite sure exactly where "here" was ...

CHAPTER 2
GOOD-BYE CIVILIZATION

"There's no way I'm going back through that hole in the cliff," said Vanessa shakily.

"We won't return that way," Mr. Prentice reassured them. "There'll be another way out of this valley. We just have to find it."

"Is this place some kind of aviary?" asked Hoover, pointing toward a patch of tall grasses. "There's no shortage of birds." An array of colorful birds had surrounded the group, strutting and hopping as they pecked the ground.

"They're so tame and so ... different!" said Elle.

Mr. Prentice looked around the valley, squinting up at the canopy of mist above them. "I've read about these kinds of places," he said. "There are some environments that have been cut off from civilization."

"Cut off?" asked Marta. "I don't get it."

"That crevice in the cliff is practically invisible," explained Mr. Prentice. "Its steep sides mean that even climbers are unlikely to see it. And this valley can't be seen by air because it's drenched in mist. What a rare type of place—it's almost impossible to discover!"

"*Unless* you have a freak accident like we did," finished Hoover.

"These birds probably roamed the whole country once," said Mr. Prentice. "I bet they're extinct everywhere but here."

"Okay, but how do we get out?" asked Marta in a very small voice.

"Good question," answered Mr. Prentice. "It's usually wise in these situations to follow the river, so let's see where this one takes us."

Fallen trees, moss-covered boulders, and low, scraggly bushes made traveling alongside the river extremely tricky. When the tangle of bushes finally gave way to low grass, everyone heaved a sigh of relief, until Vanessa glanced up ahead.

"M-M-Mr. Prentice?" she stammered. "I think we've got problems—big ones."

"It's a herd of ... of ..." Elle was speechless. There were no words to describe the enormous beasts standing between them and the other side of a wide, grassy clearing. The problem of what to perform for the school play suddenly seemed insignificant.

Mr. Prentice was looking intently at the creatures. "Don't be too hasty," he consoled the group. "It's extremely unlikely that these are meat eaters. They certainly don't eat birds, or there wouldn't be so many flightless species coexisting in the valley."

"They might eat people," worried Marta.

"I don't think so." Mr. Prentice shook his head. "Look, the one closest to us is yawning. Observe its teeth and you'll see they're short and broad, perfect for grinding up vegetation."

"I guess you'd need sharp teeth if you were a meat eater," offered Elle.

Mr. Prentice nodded. "I'm certain they're herbivores. See how they use their long necks to reach the leaves high up in the trees?"

"*And* bend all the way down to graze on grass," added Elle.

But Marta was adamant. "I still don't want to go near them."

"We *certainly* don't want to go near any of them," agreed Mr. Prentice. "Even plant eaters can be dangerous if disturbed. Big animals can move very fast when they want to, and they might see us as potential tormentors, threats to their food or their young. I'm sure they'll be very protective, and if these beasts charged us, we wouldn't stand a chance."

Mr. Prentice scanned the clearing, obviously thinking hard. "What we need to do is move stealthily around the clearing's perimeter until we encounter the river again on the other side."

The group began to edge around the clearing—everyone except Elle, that is. "What are you waiting for?" whispered Marta. "Let's go, Elle."

But Elle had something on her mind. "Mr. Prentice," she asked hesitantly, "are you really a drama teacher?"

"*What*?" said Vanessa and Hoover at the same time.

"It's just that you know a tremendous amount about science and the environment but not so much ..."

"I guess you've found me out, Elle," Mr. Prentice replied. "I'm really a science teacher, but there were no science positions available, so I applied to be the drama teacher. The school offered me the position on a temporary basis."

Vanessa's mouth dropped wide open.

"I go to lots of plays!" said Mr. Prentice quickly. "And I really enjoy the theater. It's just that ..."

"You don't know a whole lot about teaching drama?" suggested Elle gently.

Mr. Prentice nodded, eyes downcast.

Elle sighed and started walking. Everything was beginning to make sense.

CHAPTER 3
STRANGE BUT WONDERFUL

"Oh, great!" groaned Vanessa, when they arrived at the other side of the clearing. "This is exactly what we *don't* need!" Hoover tested the swampy ground facing them and sank up to his thighs in mud. "It's deep! There's no way we can get through this."

"But we're in the narrowest part of the valley," Elle pointed out. "This swamp extends to both sides of the valley walls." As everyone stood together glumly, a strange animal sploshed loudly into the rushes beside them.

"Did you guys see what I just saw?" yelped Marta. "How can something so big move so fast?"

"Or move across the swamp's surface without submerging—like me!" said Hoover indignantly.

"How does it *do* that?" asked Elle.

"It's developed wide, webbed feet to survive in the swamp," answered Mr. Prentice. "Which gives me an idea."

He gestured toward a nearby plant laden with giant leathery leaves. "We'll use the straps from our life jackets to bind these 'flippers' onto our feet."

When they had all fashioned swamp shoes for themselves, Mr. Prentice said, "Now, let's practice the swamp kangaroo leap!"

Marta had a natural talent for swamp jumping and even took the lead. Before long, the group was actually having fun.

"Woo-hoo! Here I come!" laughed Vanessa, splashing behind Elle, who was giggling so hard she almost lurched off balance.

"The swamp is changing," said Mr. Prentice a short while later. "There's more water, and I can hear the river up ahead."

Soon they were wading through a stream that gradually transformed into a narrow river.

"It would be a lot faster if we hitched a ride on one of these driftwood logs," observed Mr. Prentice.

"Are you going to help us choose the log, Hoover?" asked Mr. Prentice.

But Hoover was frozen to the spot. "This valley is so … so weird," he began. "What if we've somehow been swept into a totally different universe and there is no way back?"

For a moment, Mr. Prentice looked concerned, but then he looked closely at his watch, before glancing up at the sun and then examining the ground in front of him. "Astronomy to the rescue!" he laughed, pointing to the faint outline of his shadow on the ground. "Look, my watch says it's 12:30. The only time of day when my shadow could be that short is midday! Hoover, it's our sun up there. We're in our own wonderful world—it's just a little stranger than we thought."

Relaxed now, they threaded the straps back into their life jackets and buckled them. Then they chose one of the logs, pushed it into the water, and held on tightly.

"Kick!" ordered Mr. Prentice.

The far end of the valley loomed closer. The group left the river and walked, but soon, they could go no further. A high rock wall, draped in long red-fruited vines, prevented their passage. Beneath the vines, the river disappeared into a hole in the rock with a hollow gurgle.

"It's nothing like the rapids at the other end of the valley," said Vanessa hopefully.

"But still swift enough to thwart predators entering or animals leaving," said Mr. Prentice. "Wait here, all of you. I'm going to take a look."

Mr. Prentice pulled hard on one of the vines that trailed down into the water to make sure it would hold his weight. Then, gripping the vine tightly, he vanished into the hole. After a few minutes, the vine twitched and Mr. Prentice reappeared, hauling himself hand over hand along the vine. "It's relatively simple to follow the river's route," he declared. "All we have to do is hold on to a strong vine, which will stop us from being carried along too quickly."

"Very resourceful, Mr. P," grinned Elle. "Did science help you figure that out?"

One by one, they swung through the wall of vines. Escorted by their teacher, the children floated through the cave and emerged from the darkness.

"There's the river we *should* have taken!" Hoover pointed at the familiar fork.

"Now we'll just follow it back to camp," said Mr. Prentice.

Elle smiled at her teacher. "You're a great leader."

"Pity I'm not also a great drama teacher, then *all* our problems would be solved. I can't help you devise a script or teach you how to act." He shook his head in defeat. "We'll have to cancel the play."

Elle was silent for a moment, then she burst out laughing. "You won't have to cancel," she explained. "We have a play already! We have the lines, and we've even had the dress rehearsal. The play is called *Journey into the Valley of the Unknown*, and it's about a group of kids who are swept away and find themselves in a secret valley. When they finally find their way home, no one believes what they've seen!"

Marta, Hoover, and Vanessa punched the air. "Brilliant!" they cheered simultaneously.

"Great problem solving, Elle!" exclaimed Mr. Prentice, grinning widely. "You're thinking like a scientist!"

Respond to Reading

Summarize

Use important details from *In Drama Valley* to summarize the story. Your graphic organizer may help you.

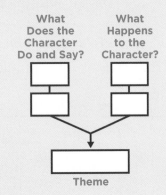

Text Evidence

1. What features of *In Drama Valley* help you identify it as a fantasy? **GENRE**

2. How can you tell that Mr. Prentice knows about nature? How does his use of this knowledge help communicate the theme of *In Drama Valley*? **THEME**

3. What is the meaning of *herbivores* on page 9? What comparisons in the text help explain its meaning? **CONTEXT CLUES: COMPARISON**

4. How does Elle's opinion of Mr. Prentice change from the beginning to the end of the story? Write about how this change supports the theme. **WRITE ABOUT READING**

Compare Texts

Read about a scientist whose knowledge of nature is helping fight disease.

Medicine from the Sea

When Professor Bill Fenical goes scuba diving in the ocean, he enters what has been called "Neptune's Medicine Chest." He and his students bring samples of marine life back to their laboratory. Here they can extract chemicals from the samples. They are hoping to discover something that can help fight diseases that have not yet been cured. Fenical wants to find a cure for cancer, and he is looking under the sea for answers!

A number of animals and plants use chemicals to prevent other animals or organisms from attacking them. The skunk is an example of a land animal that does this. Fenical's marine research uses this knowledge.

Dr. William Fenical

Bill Fenical is a researcher specializing in natural marine products. He also loves to scuba dive.

When Bill was 12 years old, he went on a trip to Florida. While he was there, he became fascinated by the ocean. Soon after that trip, his family moved to California, where he learned to scuba dive. Fenical studied organic chemistry, and he received a PhD from the University of California.

Fenical's passion for the ocean has led to a career as a leading scientist. He uses the skills gained in his hobby in his work, collecting plant and animal samples from the ocean. And the ocean is still the place where he relaxes and has fun. He even owns a boat and loves to go fishing.

Dr. Fenical (right) and an assistant study samples in the laboratory.

Fenical is interested in the chemicals that some sea animals and plants use to protect themselves. He already knows that underwater plants use chemicals to ward off attacks from bacteria and viruses, and he has devoted his career to figuring out how to use these chemicals to improve our health.

Finding a cure for cancer is a complex problem. Fenical's laboratory has found and tested two chemicals that seem to protect against the growth of some types of cancer. He found one of the chemicals in bacteria that were living in mud at the bottom of the ocean. The other chemical came from a fungus that lives on seaweed. These new-found chemicals are being tested on patients to see if they will help the patients in their fight against cancer. If the chemicals work against cancer, Fenical hopes to cultivate them in the laboratory.

Make Connections

What specific knowledge from nature helps Dr. Fenical in his search to find cures for diseases? **ESSENTIAL QUESTION**

Compare the ways Mr. Prentice in *In Drama Valley* and Dr. Fenical in *Medicine from the Sea* use their knowledge of nature to help others. **TEXT TO TEXT**

Focus on Genre

Fantasy Fantasy is a type of fiction in which other worlds can exist. There are different kinds of fantasy, from those set in ancient worlds with dragons and treasures, to modern stories in which characters go back or forward in time or change size or shape.

In some fantasies, present-day humans enter another reality through a portal, such as a mysterious train platform or a crevice in a cliff. The human characters may change shape or size, and have to cope with being in a very different world.

Read and Find Reread page 5 of *In Drama Valley* to see how Mr. Prentice and the students entered the portal to another world. Read the descriptions of the valley and the dangers to the group to see how the author created a fantasy world. On pages 14 and 15, Mr. Prentice guides the group back into the real world.

Your Turn

Work with others or by yourself to draw, illustrate, and label a map of the valley. You'll need to reread the story to make sure you've included four or more features of the valley, including the portals the characters went through.